AFTER HOURS

AFTER HOURS

30 SESSIONS FOR OUT-OF-SCHOOL CLUBS FOR 9-14 YEAR OLDS

ROB HURD

kevin
mayhew

First published in 2003 by
KEVIN MAYHEW LTD
Buxhall, Stowmarket, Suffolk IP14 3BW
E-mail: info@kevinmayhewltd.com

9 8 7 6 5 4 3 2 1 0

ISBN 1 84417 014 4
Catalogue number 1500564

Cover design by Angela Selfe
Edited and typeset by Elisabeth Bates
Printed in Great Britain

Contents

About the author

Rob Hurd has worked for 11 years as a schools worker and youth worker. He worked in Lutterworth, Leicestershire for two years from September 1989 to 1991. He set up and ran a schools team called 'Lifeline', regularly visiting all the junior and secondary schools in the area to take assemblies, and he ran two Christian Unions. He also worked as a council youth worker and church youth/children worker at that time, organising a variety of youth events and missions.

In 1993 he started working for 'In Christ in School' as a secondary school worker and youth worker, regularly visiting 20 middle and upper comprehensive schools to take assemblies, lessons, and lunchtime and after-school clubs. He also organises a youth weekend each year called 'Spotlight' in which he and a team of volunteers take away approximately 100 young people to Derbyshire for a whole range of activities. He runs youth clubs, organises and speaks at youth events, churches, holiday clubs and school workers' meetings.

Rob Hurd can be contacted at robjhurd@hotmail.com

Acknowledgements

Thanks to . . .

Jesus for giving me a sense of humour, a desire to have fun, and the opportunity to use both these throughout the years in the different lunchtime, after-school and youth clubs; also for inspiring and anointing me so that I could use the different games and activities as a tool for telling all young people about the difference Christ can make in their lives, and enabling them to think about the issues that relate to them.

Hazel Brittain for typing all this out.

Dave Witham, 'In Christ In School' treasurer, for paying my expenses for some of the equipment I have bought, which may have seemed a bit suspect, such as – lipstick, shaving foam, tights, yoghurts, flour, marshmallows and millions of sweets!

Julie, my wife, for washing loads of sheets and towels over the years that were covered in things such as flour, yoghurt and eggs, some of which had been left in my car boot for a week!

The various schools that have been very happy for us to run these clubs, and been supportive to us.

Foreword

I hope that this book can be of help to you in your work in schools or your youth club. All the games in it have been tried and tested over 11 years and have proved to work well. Some of the games may need certain pieces of equipment, but most of these you will find in your equipment cupboard if you have one or at home, so they should not be too hard to get. The themes and games may be used with un-churched young people, in the 9-14 age range.

On more than one occasion I have had a gang of tough, hardened teenagers taking part in a game of 'Get knotted' which some teenagers would initially be too embarrassed to do. So these games can work!

All the games are linked to themes that will encourage the group to believe in themselves and think about moral and ethical questions that affect them. They will learn how much God loves them and can make a difference in their lives.

So have a read. Adapt the themes and games to your situation and have some fun.

ROB HURD

Introduction

Promoting your after-school or lunchtime club

In order to draw young people to your lunchtime or after-school club you need to catch their interest. So, instead of going to the front of the hall in an assembly and saying: 'I would like to give an announcement about the lunchtime/after-school club that we run. It's on this particular day, at this time, in this room, and we do these things . . . please come along for loads of fun . . .' how about using this rap to make the announcement?

It might not work, but then again it might, and once you've got the kids, *After Hours* is on hand to provide ideas for running your sessions!

Welcome to . . .

I was walking down the corridor past room nine
when I looked at the door and I saw the sign,
'If you want some fun, and plenty to do,
come on through and we'll entertain you.'

There were two lads sitting with cream on their face,
some girls with water having a race.
Squirt it about and make a mess
with eggs and yoghurt, cream and chocolate,
any food, more or less.

We do some juggling and play wacky games,
fun and laughter are our aims.
With drama, quizzes and stories each week
it's your happiness that we seek.

We'll talk about life and what it's about.
Issues and worries that make you shout.

Learn from the Bible . . . and Jesus too,
you never know, he might help you.
He's always there, and he's a great friend;
on his power we can all depend.
If you wanna believe
or Christ receive,
that's really great, but there's no force,
we're not here for some great cause.

So what we wanna say is come on through,
whoever you are we welcome you.
We'll have some fun
and we'll plan to do what you want to do.

What lies ahead? - New Year

Aim

To show that we don't know what the future may hold for us – but we do know *who* holds the future.

Game

Play your cards right

Display approximately 40 playing cards in two rows of 20 with a gap in the middle, face down on a table or with Blu-Tack on a wall. Divide the group into two teams. Both teams face the cards. From each team choose a volunteer to be the 'contestant'. To play the game you ask both contestants a question. The one who gets it right can play the game. You turn over the first card and they have to decide whether the next card is higher or lower. Their team can shout out what they think. If they guess right they move on to the next card and continue until they win. If they guess wrong then you ask another question to both contestants or just let the other contestant have a go. For this game ACE can be high or low. The contestants can swap only two cards and cards of equal number don't count, it has to be higher or lower.

Talk

Explain that when you are playing the game you never know what the next card will be. You have to make the right decision to win. You never know how it will turn out until you turn the card over. In the same way at the start of a new year (or term) you never know what may happen in a week or a month. No one knows what the future holds, or how a situation we are in, whether good or bad, will turn out. But, one thing that we do know is *who* holds the future – Jesus.

Bible bit

Divide the group into two teams. One team is to act out the story of Joseph who was taken as a slave into Egypt (Genesis 37:12-26). The other team is to act out how he became a great official (Genesis 41:1-43). God knew his future, he had a plan for him and was with him.

Game

The story unfolds

Get the group into two or three circles depending on the numbers and give them each a pen. The first person in the group has to write on a piece of paper, 'Once upon a time there was a ....' and they can write anything down. They then fold the paper over and the next person writes down their name and where they live folding it down again. The next person writes down what they like doing, etc. Give each person in the circle something to write down, for instance, name, address, hobbies, what he saw or did that day. After you get to the last person in the circle, read out the story and see how the story turns out! It will be very funny.

Talk

Explain that sometimes situations in life seem ridiculous. We ask, 'Can this really be happening?' But not only does God know our future and have a plan for our lives, he also is with us when things go wrong. Just like Joseph, God will never leave us because he loves us.

Priorities

Aim

To show that some things in life are really important, for instance, school and family. We need to remember those important things in our lives.

Games

Shops

Place around the room five pieces of card with the following written on them – School, Chemist, Church, Supermarket, and Leisure centre. Get the entire group to stand in the middle of the room. Then shout out items you would find in each place. They have to run to the specific place. The last person to get there is out. Say that all of these places are important: Leisure centre – fitness/fun. School – education. Chemist – health. Church – spirituality. Supermarket – food. We need all of these things in life.

Conveyer belt

Get a tray and fill it with lots of objects (30-50). Everyone stands up and looks at the tray of objects for ten seconds then you cover it up again. Get the group into teams and have them write down as many objects as they can remember. Explain that we need to remember the important things in life.

Group activity

Divide the group into pairs and give them a pen and paper. They have five minutes to write down in numerical order the ten most important things they would get out of their house if it were on fire. Read out each list, then discuss what people saw as important and why.

Bible bit

Read the story of the rich young ruler from Matthew 19:16-30.

Talk

Explain that when the rich young ruler met Jesus he thought he had everything in life, and that he had his life sorted out, but he felt empty. Only by following Jesus and being willing to give up his possessions would he get complete satisfaction. It is the same for us; if we put our trust in Jesus he will show us what is important in life.

Life's a team

Aim

To show that in life we need to work with other people. It's important to be able to work together and help each other.

Team games

Balloon pass

Two teams are needed. They stand in two lines. The person at the front of each line passes a balloon to the next person – the balloon is passed knee to knee to the end and back again. The first team to do this win. Then the two teams do it again but as the balloon is going down the line knee to knee, another balloon is being passed chin to chin in the other direction. The winning team is the one that passes both balloons up and down the lines first.

Polo pass

Have two or three teams, depending on numbers. Each team member has a straw in his or her mouth. They have to pass a polo along the team straw to straw. The winning team is the one who can pass the polo along as quickly as possible.

Story

Tell the story of Nehemiah who organised the building of the walls of Jerusalem.

Talk

It is so important to work together as a team. LIFE! We need to help each other and work with others. Talk about the importance of working together, helping each other and being nice.

Game

Blindfolded yoghurt eat

Get six volunteers and blindfold three of them. The other three have to race and feed yoghurt as fast as possible to their partner. The first team to empty their yoghurt pot are the winners. Play this game to emphasise a team working together.

The ordinary things

Aim

To show that God can use us for his glory – he uses ordinary people to do his work.

Games

What job?
Divide the group into two teams. Choose a volunteer from each team to stand at the front. When they are at the front give them a career which they have to mime out. It could be a tree surgeon, street cleaner, policeman or anything else. The first team to guess correctly wins a point and then the next two volunteers have a go. See which team win overall.

Improvisation
Divide the group into teams of four or five and give each team about ten ordinary objects and a short story which they have to act out, using the ordinary objects as visual aids for the story. See which team uses the objects in the funniest and most imaginative way to do the drama. Stories could be – 'I went on holiday and this happened' or 'I was walking through the fields and this happened'. You will need 10-15 minutes for this game.

Bible bit

Tell the story of Gideon – how he was an ordinary man, nothing special, but God used him for his glory in an amazing way.

Talk

Explain that God can use us in amazing ways if we will let him. We don't have to be superstars to be used by God – he chooses the ordinary things of the world (as in the Improvisation game) to shame the wise, the weak to shame the strong, just as he used Gideon. It does not matter what job we have God can use us to talk about our faith in him. He can give us gifts for his glory if we will let him. Have faith and do what he tells you to do.

Game

Give each person a piece of newspaper. They have five minutes to carefully tear the paper into long strips and see who can make the longest strip. If it is done carefully it can be really long. Lay them down on the floor to see who has the longest strip.

Conclusion

Tell the group that it is amazing how you can get a really long strip from an ordinary piece of newspaper. God can use you in amazing ways as well.

Temptation

Aim

To show that we all get tempted to do wrong at some point in our lives but we must try to resist temptation.

Games

Tug-of-war

Divide the group into two teams facing each other. Give each team member a number and place a rope in the middle of the room with two objects such as traffic cones at each end of the room. Then shout a number. The two team members with that number have to run and grab an end of the rope and pull the other team member towards their cone. If it goes on a long time, call out another number to help them.

Dodge ball

Divide the group into two teams. One team stands in the middle of the room; the other team forms a circle around them. The team on the outside has to throw balls (not too hard!) at the inside team. If they hit someone that person is out. The inside team has to try to dodge the balls. This goes on until all the team is out, then they change places.

Story

Jesus tempted by the devil: explain that even Jesus was tempted by the devil but he resisted. As in the game Tug-of-war you might feel pulled towards something you know is wrong, but don't let the devil drag you into doing something wrong. Ask God to give you the strength to resist and he will! As in the game Dodge ball try to dodge sin by praying 'Lord lead me not into temptation'.

Illustration

Get a McDonald's milk shake as a prize but without telling the group. Put anything disgusting that you can find in it like mud, stones, dirt, chewing gum, etc. Then offer it to a volunteer. Just before they go to drink it tell them that it looks lovely, but inside it's not really nice. Explain that temptation is like that – it looks nice with all of its attractive coverings but deep down it's not at all what you thought it would be.

Pride comes before a . . .

Aim

To show that some people are too proud of themselves and feel that they are better than anyone else. Don't be too proud but treat other people as you would treat yourself.

Games

Balloon float

Give each member of the group a balloon that they need to blow up and tie a knot in. When they have done that the game starts. All they have to do is stand in a specified space and without holding onto their own balloon keep it afloat by tapping it and at the same time trying to knock the others' balloons to the floor. If someone's balloon touches the floor it can be burst and that person is out. The winner is the last member with their balloon afloat.

Balloon burst

Give each member a balloon which they have to blow up, tie a knot in and tie to their shoe lace (or ankle if they don't have laces). On the word 'GO' everyone can try and stamp on the others' balloons whist protecting their own (both feet must be on the floor). The winner is the one with their balloon intact.

Story

Tell the story of the Tower of Babel (Genesis 11:1-9). Explain how the people were too proud and built an enormous tower to make a name for themselves and how God scattered all the people.

Talk

Explain that sometimes pride can be dangerous: in the first game the idea was to keep your own balloon high up in the air and at the same time knocking the other balloons down. The second game was also about your own survival at everyone else's expense. Sometimes we are like that; we think that we are higher or better than others but in God's eyes we are all equally precious! We need to see others as valuable and precious as ourselves.

Game

Funnel game

Get two or three volunteers who have a good sense of humour. Give them a coin and a funnel each. Tell them to put the funnel in the top of their trousers and the coin on their foreheads. At the word 'GO' they have to nod their heads and try and drop the coin into the funnel. Explain that the funnel is in their trousers so they can't cheat by moving it. After two attempts, as they lean their heads backwards to try again, pour water into their funnels! Use this game to re-emphasise that it is not nice being tricked by someone or getting wet! We need to treat each other fairly and not try to get the better of them.

Problems

Aim

To show that we all have problems but God understands and can help us if we trust in him.

Group activity

Bring in newspapers or magazines and get the group to find articles where things have gone wrong – disasters or human tragedies. Mention something from a newspaper/TV where something bad has happened in the world or with someone famous. Say that from time to time we all have problems and often think there is no way out *but* there is!!

Talk

Explain that we all have problems. Sometimes things go wrong in our lives, situations don't work out as we had planned. Sometimes we face difficulties and feel that we can't cope and there is no way out. The good news is that whatever situations we face, however bad it may seem, often there is a light at the end of the tunnel. It's good to remember that whatever we go through, God can help us. He loves us and knows what it is to suffer.

Games

Get knotted

Divide everyone into groups of six to eight people. They stand in a circle and cross hands with someone opposite. Now get out of this mess without letting go of each other's hands and form a circle again. Explain that problems are often too hard to get out of but not if we put our lives into God's hands. If you ask God to help you he will.

Card house

Everyone gets into groups of three or four. They are given loads of playing cards and have to try and build the highest card house. Give about five minutes to play this game.

Story

Tell the story of the wise and foolish builders. The one who built his house on sand had problems; the rains came and the house crashed. The one who built his house on the rock was safe; his house was firm and strong. So build your life on Christ.

Talk

Talk about how important it is to follow Jesus and read the Bible. Pray and trust in him. Stand strong in your faith so that when problems come you can stand firm and God will help you.

Love your enemies

Aim

To show that it is easy to hate someone or knock them down verbally and physically but being nice is better.

Game

Gladiator challenge
Give two volunteers a pillow each. They have to stand on one leg and hit each other with the pillows till one of them loses by putting their foot down. Keep going until all the group have had a go.

Talk

It is easy to knock others down by calling them names or bullying them but it can really harm and hurt them. Ask if anyone has been bullied or picked on. Show an article/story about a tragic victim of bullying and say how it affected them. We need to work together and help each other.

Story

In three groups act out the story of the good Samaritan from Luke 10:25-37. Let the group choose their own characters then watch the three plays.

Game

Get up
Get everyone into groups of six. Each group has two people sitting on the floor, back to back, linking arms and with legs out in front. They have to get up without letting go of each other's arms. When

they have done that (practise first), the third person joins them, then the fourth, fifth and the sixth. The winner is the first group with all six linking arms and getting up.

Conclusion

It is better to work together and help each other rather than knock each other down.

Friendship

Aim

To show the importance of friendship and that it means being kind and supportive and accepting one another no matter what.

Games

Signature bingo

Give each person a sheet of paper with boxes drawn on it, one box for each person present. Then they have to go around each person and get them to sign their name in any single box until they have all the signatures. When that is done call out the names of all present and as you do so the person can tick off that name. The winners are those who have a line of boxes with names that have been called out and crossed off.

Foot signature

Give each person a pen. They have five minutes to collect as many signatures on their feet as possible. The winner is the one with most signatures.

Friendship

Divide the group into twos or threes and give them pen and paper. They have three minutes to write down as many qualities of friendship as possible.

Talk

It was nice to have a lot of signatures in the first two games. It would be great if we had as many friends as signatures! Friendship is important. Refer to some of the qualities that make a good friend and point out that commitment and loyalty are really important.

Bible bit

Read from Matthew 26:47-56, 69-75 about how Jesus' friend Judas betrayed him and how Jesus was rejected by all of his friends when he was arrested and judged. Explain that Jesus knew what it was like to lose one's friends. Therefore the best qualities of friendship are commitment, loyalty and support. Have that and you will have friends for life.

Heroes

Aim

To show that Jesus is an amazing person – a real hero, not a wimp. He was intelligent, courageous and the Son of God

Game

Divide the group into pairs and give them pen and paper. In their pairs ask them to write down as many heroes or famous actors as possible – especially hard, tough men or women.

Talk

Discuss one famous film star that was named on their paper (such as Arnie, Jean Claude Van Damme or Bruce Willis). Ask what it is that makes them famous and then write down the answers. (It should be characteristics as well as looks.)

Game

Pictionary

Divide the group into two teams. Each team has to choose a volunteer to go up to the front. Give them a famous character whom they have to draw on the flip chart. The team that guesses the character first wins. After doing a few characters get them to draw Jesus. You can guarantee that the only symbol they can think of is to draw the cross.

Talk

Explain that Jesus is the greatest hero ever, more so than the famous heroes the groups have just written down and also that he is God! Read out the story of when Jesus calmed the storm. Mention that he also had thousands of followers, he walked right through a mob that was trying to throw him off a cliff, and he turned the tables in the temple. He was tough, intelligent, witty, etc., and was brave enough to die the most awful death – because he loved us.

Sin – say 'no'

Aim

To show that we all do wrong (sin) but Jesus loves us and can forgive us if we put our trust in him.

Games

Stick in the mud

Everyone runs around the room. Two volunteers have some footballs. They have to throw the balls at the others. If they hit them below the knee then that person cannot move at all until they are set free by one of the others crawling between their feet.

I say

Everyone has to do exactly what you say but only when you say 'I say'. If they do something and you didn't say 'I say' they are out. If you say 'I say' – put your hands in the air–and they don't do it then they are out. Explain that often instead of doing what is right, we follow the crowd.

Yes/No

Get a volunteer and talk to them. Ask them questions, but they must not answer with yes or no. See if they can last one minute.

Talk

Like the game 'I say' we all make mistakes and do our own things in life rather that doing what is right by following God's commands. We all mess up, or sin, as the Bible calls it. It is easy to say yes to doing wrong but very difficult to say no, like the last game. The great news is that God sent Jesus to die on the cross for us and set us free, as in the game Stick in the mud. He can set us free if we ask for his forgiveness and follow him.

Easter: he's alive

Aim

To show that not only did Christ die on the cross for our forgiveness – but three days later he came back again.

Games

Clay modelling

Divide the group into teams of two or three. Give each team a lump of clay. They have ten minutes to make as many different objects as possible out of the clay – but they have to get your approval that each object is a reasonable representation before they can carry on making another object. See which team can make the most objects in ten minutes.

Picture puzzle

Whilst still in their teams give them a poster and a pair of scissors. (Any poster will do.) Also give them a roll of sticky tape. They have to cut the poster up into fifty pieces! After that give them ten minutes to put their poster back together using the sticky tape and see which team can get the best poster again.

Bible bit

Act or read out Luke 24:12 where it tells about Christ's resurrection.

Talk

Pick up one of the clay objects and one of the reconstructed posters. Explain that it is amazing how often you can remodel a clay object.

The clay was smashed down, thumped, kneaded and pinched, yet some amazing objects have come out of it. As for the poster – it did look nice, but now, even though it has been stuck back together it still looks a mess.

Compare those objects to Jesus – he was smashed, thumped, pinched, knocked about and killed and yet amazingly he rose again from death to life. He had a new form, unlike the poster that was cut into pieces and proved impossible to make as new. When something like this is broken it often cannot be fixed properly, yet Jesus was brought to life by the power of God.

Acceptance

Aim

To show that we need to accept each other and be nice to each other, not be prejudiced. Being rejected can hurt, so think about how you treat each other.

Games

Piggy in the middle
Divide the group into teams of about ten people. Each team stands in a circle facing inward. One of the team then stands in the middle of the circle and the others have to pass a ball to each other for as long as possible without letting the person in the middle getting hold of the ball. See who is quickest at getting the ball whilst in the middle.

Musical numbers
Play some decent modern music and get everybody to walk around the room. When the music stops call out a number. They then have to get into groups of that number as quickly as possible. All those who are not in groups of the right number are out.

Story

Tell the story of Joseph from Genesis 37:12-36 about how his brothers rejected him, threw him into a pit and then sold him as a slave.

Talk

Speak to one of the group and say that it is not nice being rejected. In the first game everyone had the ball and would not pass it to the one in the middle, which is sad. The second game was even worse because when it came to the crunch even so-called 'friends' pushed you away so that they could win. It's not very nice being rejected. Joseph felt the same when his brothers rejected him! We need to accept one another – no matter what they look like, their character or their culture.

Game

Mummy game
Get two volunteers to stand still. Two other volunteers are given a roll of toilet paper. They have two minutes to wrap their team mate up. The winner is the one who does the best 'mummy'.

Story

Tell the story of Jesus from Luke 17:11-19, when he healed the men with leprosy. Explain that they would have been wrapped up in bandages as in the last game; everyone rejected them for fear of catching the leprosy. Yet Jesus went near them and touched them and healed them. Jesus loves you as well and will not reject you!

Listening to your conscience

Aim

To show that we need to understand our conscience, and to listen to it.

Games

Wink murder

Everyone sits in a circle. One person goes out of the room while the rest of the group chooses someone to be a murderer. When the person (the detective) comes back into the room he has to guess who the murderer is. He/she has three chances to guess. The murderer has to wink at everyone individually, causing that person to scream and lie down. The game goes on until the detective catches out the murderer or everyone is dead.

Guess the conductor

The group sit in a circle while one person goes out of the room. That person has to be the 'critic'. The group then decides who in the group should be the conductor. The critic then comes into the room and stands in the middle of the circle. As they do so the conductor has to mime the playing of a musical instrument. Everyone else in the group has to follow suit. The critic has three chances to guess who the conductor is.

What's that?

Divide the group into two teams. Then play a tape with lots of different sound effects on. The two teams have to guess what the noises are. The team that gets the most right is the winner.

Talk

The aim of Wink murder is for the murderer to try and 'kill people' for as long as possible without getting caught. In the same way the 'conductor' has to lead the group for as long as possible without getting caught. If we are honest we all do things wrong and we try to get away with it. We need to stop and think, 'Is this right, should I be doing this?' This is our conscience at work. Like the sound-effects game we need to understand and listen to our conscience. Ask if anyone has done something wrong which he or she knew they should not have done.

Story

Tell the story of Jonah who did everything wrong and tried to get away from God for as long as he could. In the end his conscience got the better of him and he said 'sorry' to God and did what was right.

Conclusion

Do what is right – understanding your conscience is important but more important is to listen to it.

The answer

Aim

To show that there are some things in life that we don't understand or know the answer to, but we shouldn't worry about this as we can't know everything. What we do need to know is that Jesus is the answer.

Games

Scissor pass

Everyone gets into a circle. The leader holds a pair of scissors and passes them to the pupil on their left. As the leader passes them they say 'I pass these scissors to you uncrossed'. The pupil then has to pass the scissors to the person on their left and say either 'I pass these scissors to you crossed' or 'I pass these scissors to you uncrossed'. The leader says whether the pupil has passed them correctly or not. The pupils have to guess how they can pass the scissors correctly. The secret is – while the person passes the scissors, if their legs are crossed then they say, 'I pass these scissors to you crossed', and if their legs are uncrossed they say, 'I pass these scissors to you uncrossed'. The pupils will think that the term crossed and uncrossed refer to the scissors which are either open (crossed) or closed (uncrossed). The winner is the person who realises that it's their legs which dictate how the scissors are passed.

It's a tick/tock

Everyone sits in a circle or two depending on numbers. Two pens go around, one is called a 'tick' and one is called a 'tock'. You pass the pen to the next person and say 'This is a tick' (the 'tock' is going around in the opposite way). The person then says 'a what?' and the person giving the pen says 'a tick'. The person who has received the pen says the same but when the next person says 'a what' the second person looks at the first person and says 'a what'. The first person says 'a tick' which is then passed on to the person receiving the tick (pen). So it's: this is a tick, a what, a what, a tick, a tick, a tick, etc. It gets very confusing, especially when the tick and the tock cross over.

Talk

Explain that there are some things in life that we don't understand; unanswered questions. As in the first game sometimes we face situations in life which are very complicated and we can't cope, we never understand everything, but the truth is that Jesus is the only answer to life, he knows everything because he is God.

Bible bit

Read out Luke 2:41 when Jesus as a child could answer all the questions of the teachers.

Puzzle

Do this puzzle with all the group. Ask them to pick a number between 1-100. Don't say what it is. Double it. Add 30, divide by half. Take away your original number. The answer is always 15.

Conclusion

Finish by saying that whilst we don't know everything we do have so much intelligence and many answers in life but we need to use our intelligence wisely to benefit, not damage, others.

Get a life!

Aim

To show that it is good to have a hobby or activity you like to do and it is important to try and achieve great things.

Games

Hit the coin

Get two volunteers out to the front. They need to stand opposite each other with a 2p coin on the floor between them. They need to throw a ball at the coin and see who is the first to hit it.

Guess the activity

Divide the group into two teams. Each team has to choose a volunteer to mime out an activity in front of the team. The first team to guess correctly wins and someone else from the team has a go. For example, fixing a bike puncture, changing a plug, making a cup of coffee.

Talk

It is good to have something to aim for in life, as in the coin game where you are aiming for a coin. Often if we want to achieve anything we need to persevere in order to achieve it. As with the mime game there are so many things we can do in life – anything is possible. We all have a gift, an ability, we just need to try hard and use our gifts.

Story

Tell the story of Nehemiah who built the walls of Jerusalem. It seemed impossible to rebuild them but Nehemiah set his goal to do it and he did. He also encouraged everyone to have a go.

Prayer

Pray and ask God to help you achieve things that you never thought were possible. For his glory.

Game

Paper plane race: Each person has a piece of paper. They have to make a paper aeroplane and draw a design on it. After everyone has done so they all stand next to each other and throw their plane. The one who reaches the furthest wins.

Play this game to emphasise that we can all achieve something. Conclude by explaining that some people may do better than others but what matters is the trying; putting your best into it is what counts.

Which side are you on?

Aim

To show that you may never know what is going to happen in life, or when it will end. But what is important is which side you are on – is it God's side? That is the best side to be on.

Games

Basketball/netball

Play a game of basketball or netball. Instead of posts use a member of each team to stand on the opposite side of their teams on chairs and be their posts. They have to catch the ball without stepping off their chair to give their team a goal. The team with the most goals wins.

Samson, Delilah, Lion

Split the group into two teams. Each team has to decide whether to be Samson (call out 'He-man'), Delilah (call out 'Oh, Samson') or the Lion (call out 'Roar'). Each team forms a line in the centre of the room and faces the other team. They act out either Samson, Delilah or the Lion, whatever their chosen character is, but Samson kills the Lion; the Lion kills Delilah, and Delilah kills Samson. As they act it out together the ones who get killed turn and run and the other team chases them and tries to catch them before they reach the end of the room. If they catch them that person joins their team.

Mention that being on the right team is very important, just as in the netball game.

Drama

Act out the story of David and Goliath from 1 Samuel 17:41-54.

Talk

Goliath seemed really tough, a real hero. The Philistines were laughing at Israel's fear, yet David, against all odds, killed him. He won as he was on the best side – God's side, because he trusted God. Being on God's side is the best side to be on – you can be if you put your trust in Jesus.

Faith

Aim

To show that if you believe in Jesus you shouldn't let the devil or people try to take your faith away.

Games

Key snatch

Get one volunteer to sit on a chair blindfolded. Give them a soft club and put some keys under the chair in the corner of the room. Group members have to try and creep up and steal the keys without being hit. If they are pointed at directly by the volunteer or hit with the club they are out. Explain that Satan will try to creep up on you and try to take away your faith.

The box

Divide the group into two teams. One team has to sit down around a large box and the other team has to stand behind them but a few feet away. The team that is standing has to throw as many tennis balls or rolls of paper into the box as possible. The other team has to defend the box and try to stop the balls or paper from going in.

Illustration

Get a long strip of paper (wallpaper can be good) about three feet long, put a twist in it and tape the two ends together to make a hoop. Explain that faith is like this hoop. Ask God to help you keep your faith and he will; there will be no end to your faith, just like the hoop. Say that if we do not do something about our faith, like praying and reading the Bible and witnessing, etc., it will stay small like our hoop. If we do something about our faith it will grow bigger. As you say this cut along the middle of the hoop all the way around and the hoop will have doubled in size.

Talk

Explain that just like the team who were throwing balls into the box, the devil and people are going to try and attack your faith, but God loves you and will help you to thwart the attack and he will defend you.

Trust

Aim

To show that it is important to trust in God – he will not let you down.

Games

Planks

Put two chairs out with a plank resting between them. Two volunteers are chosen to lift up the plank and two volunteers to stand in front of the plank. Choose two more volunteers to go out of the room, be blindfolded and come back into the room individually. The blindfolded volunteer has to stand on the plank between the chairs with their hands on the shoulders of the people standing in front of the plank. The two lifters have to lift the plank with the person on it (a leader needs to be near in case they fall). The person has to jump off the plank. BUT as the plank gets higher unknown to the jumper the two that are in front slowly lower themselves at the same time. Hence instead of being only chair-height off the ground they think that they are six feet off the ground!! Now jump! Explain about the concept of TRUST.

Chairs

Put out two lines of six chairs haphazardly. Two people are blindfolded and with the aid of a guide and a helper to stop them falling they have to walk across the chairs as quickly as possible without falling.

Talk

These games are difficult, as it is hard to trust in what you cannot see. It is the same with God, you cannot see him – so how can you trust him? *But* every day you have to trust in what you cannot see as in the following game.

Game

Blindfolded food taste

Get a few volunteers and blindfold them. They have to taste lots of food laid out in dishes and try to guess what the food is (e.g. salt, baking powder, flour, and sugar).

Talk

Every day you have to trust people who have cooked or packed food, people whom you have not seen. They may have spat in the food, you don't know. You have to trust in them without seeing. It is the same with God – you cannot see him – but you *can* trust him.

Story

Tell the story of Daniel in the lion's den from Daniel 6 – he trusted in God.

Game

Flour tower

Get four volunteers and blindfold them. They have to find three sweets hidden in bowls under piles of flour and retrieve them with their teeth! For more fun wet their faces beforehand.

Prayer

Aim

To show that God hears our prayers – we first need to talk to him.

Games

Labels

Stick a label with a famous character's name on it on the back of each person. They have to guess who they are by asking questions about the character. The person answering the questions can only answer yes or no. Explain that God knows everything about us, he knows our needs, our faults and who we are.

Chinese whispers

Divide the group into two teams. Each team sits in a circle. The first person in the circle has to whisper a long rhyme to the next person who passes it down the line. The team that is the quickest and most accurate wins.

Story

Tell the story of Elijah (from 1 Kings 18:41-46) who prayed for rain and it came. Also mention some of the things that Jesus prayed for and God answered. Such as the feeding of the 5000.

Talk

As in the first game God knows everything about us, our needs, our faults, our personalities and yet he still loves us. He can answer our prayers if we ask him. It doesn't matter about the words whether we get them mixed up like Chinese whispers but, God can still answer them if we have faith and trust him.

Prayer exercise

Divide the group into teams of two or three and write out a prayer and read it out to the group.

Life in abundance

Aim

To show that filling our lives with things may be great but it does not always make us happy. Only Jesus can give us life in all of its fullness.

Games

Peg out

Get a washing line/piece of string and tie it up in the room. Then get two or three volunteers and blindfold them. Using just one hand they have to put as many pegs on the line as possible. See who can put the most pegs on the line to win.

Chubby bunnies

Get three volunteers. They have to fill their mouths with as many marshmallows as possible and say 'chubby bunnies'. Whoever can get the most in their mouth wins.

Cola challenge

Put three types of different cola in three unlabelled bottles. Then four volunteers have to drink from them to try and work out which is the 'real' cola. Apparently Dr John Pemberton created the real cola and gave it a secret ingredient called 7X. It's the 7X that makes it different from all other colas.

Talk

The aim of Chubby bunnies was to try and fill your mouth with as many marshmallows as possible. The peg game was about getting as many pegs as you could on the line. Life is like that. A lot of people think that the only way to be happy in this life is to get as many things as possible and have as many 'pegs on the line' as possible. Some people who have been successful and rich, know that this isn't always true. Just like the cola challenge, all the colas were OK but the 'real' cola is the best because it has a secret ingredient. It is the same with Jesus. He is the secret ingredient – the only way to life in all of its fullness.

Story

Tell the story of Zacchaeus (Luke 19:1-10) or the rich young ruler (Matthew 19:16-30) to emphasise the point. Both had wealth but not happiness.

God is everywhere

Aim

To show that wherever we are God is there – he is everywhere, and nothing can separate us from his love.

Quiz

Divide the group into two teams and do a quiz about famous places in the world, such as the Eiffel Tower, Pyramids, Taj Mahal. Ask the group if they have been to any of these places, or any other interesting places. Show some photographs of different places in the world.

Games

Partners

On a table or flipchart you have a variety of cards, each one with a number on. On the other side of the card is a famous person's name. Somewhere amongst the other cards is that person's partner. The two teams take it in turns to shout out a number, see whose name is on it and find his/her partner. Find as many partners as possible till all the cards are gone. Possible partners are Adam and Eve, Robin Hood and Maid Marion, Postman Pat and Jess, Ant and Dec, Samson and Delilah.

Guess the contents

Show a jar full of sweets. Everybody has to guess how many sweets are in the jar. The one closest wins the jar of sweets.

Talk

Read out Romans 8:37-39. Nothing can separate us from the love of God. Explain that wherever we may be in the world and however many people there are, we can never escape from God's love as he is everywhere and he knows everything about us.

Which way?

Aim

To show that Jesus is the only way to have life in all its fullness. He can guide us through life if we trust in him!

Games

Map game

Divide the young people into groups of three or four. Each group is given a map. One of the group is the runner. The leader shouts a place on the map, for example a school or a landmark. The first runner to find the location and show you wins a point for their team.

Blindfold search

Divide the group into two teams. The first person in each team is blindfolded. Place on the floor two different coloured or shaped balls, one for each team. When you say 'go' the two people have to find their ball by following the commands of the rest of the team. When the player has found the ball he has to pick it up, run back to the team and the next person goes. The winning team is the one to finish first. Keep going until all the team has had a go.

Talk

Tell a story about when you have been lost, maybe whilst driving or perhaps in a town centre. A map is an essential item to have when travelling around. In the Map game maps are very important. When you get lost in a town centre there are people who can help by directing you to the place you need to be at, as in the second game. Relate this to Jesus. If we go through life on our own 'spiritually' we are bound to get lost or come to a dead end at some point, but if we have Jesus as our spiritual friend and Saviour he can help us through life.

Game

Apple bobbing

Two volunteers are blindfolded, the others have to tell them where the apples are in two bowls of water. The winner is the first to find the apple and pick it up with their teeth. Play this to emphasise the point about being guided.

Aaah – to be at the seaside

Aim

To show how even holidays can make us think of Jesus.

Games

Captain's deck

The group stands in the middle of the room. Point at the four corners of the room and give them the name of a 'room' found on a boat, i.e cabin, engine room, mess room. As you shout out the name of a room the group has to run to that 'room'. When they know which room is in which corner add a few commands which they have to follow:

Scrub the deck – they scrub the floor.
Up the rigging – they climb a ladder (mime)
Captain's coming – salute
Crow's Nest – use binoculars
Bombs overhead – fall to the floor
Man overboard – Get into twos and piggy back

The idea is to shout out a command which they have to follow, the last one to do so is out. At the same time as shouting out commands you can shout a 'room'. The winner is the one that is left.

Beachcombers

Divide the group into two teams. One team are the 'beachcombers' and the other team is the 'tide'. They stand facing each other at two ends of the room. Give each team member a number. In the middle are about 20 objects on the floor. What you have to do is shout a number and an object; the 'beachcomber' with that number has to try and get the particular object and take it back to his team without the tide touching him. If he is touched then he has to drop the object. After a few minutes see how many objects have been successfully picked up by the 'beachcombers'. Swap the teams around so that the 'tide' becomes the 'beachcombers' and 'beachcombers' become the 'tide'. See if they can pick up more objects.

Bible bit

Read or act out Luke 5:1-11 where Jesus asked his disciples to cast their fishing nets again and they caught a large number of fish.

Game

Kipper fan race
Divide the group into two teams. The teams need to stand behind each other in two lines. The two team members at the front of the line are given a newspaper and a piece of paper cut into the shape of a fish. On the word go they have to use the newspaper to fan the fish as quickly as possible into a bucket on its side on the other side of the room. When the fish has been fanned into the bucket the team member runs back to their team and the next person goes. Continue until all the team members have had a go and you have a winning team.

Talk

Ask the group what these games have in common. All of these games are to do with the seaside. Tell them, when they go on holiday, to remember the Bible reading/drama how Jesus was beside the water's edge and he commanded his disciples to obey him (as in the Captain's deck game). Like the Kipper fan race this seemed really impossible: how could they catch so many fish? But Jesus did a miracle because he is the Son of God. Like his disciples, if we obey him and have faith in Jesus he can do miracles in our lives.

Creation

Aim

To show that God has created a beautiful world and we need to do more to keep it that way.

Games

Earth, sea, animal

Put 3 pieces of card around the room with the words Earth, Sea and Animal on them. Ask the group to stand in the middle of the room. Then shout out an item found in either the sea, or the land or the name of an animal. The group has to run to the appropriate card. The last one to get there loses.

Fruit salad

Ask the group to sit down in a circle. Walk around the circle and give each person the name of one of four types of fruit. The four fruits can be Apple, Pear, Orange, Banana. Someone shouts out one of the fruits. As they do so all those who are that fruit must stand up and run around the circle. The last one to get back to their place is out. After a few tries shout out 'Change' whilst some are still running around. This means they have to change direction. You can also shout out 'Fruit salad'. This means that the whole group has to stand up and run around the circle and sit down. Play the game until you have a winner.

Alphabet activity

Divide the group into teams of three or four. Give each team a pen and paper. They have to write each letter of the alphabet on the paper. On the word 'go' they have to write down something that has been created (not made by humans) which begins with that letter. See who can get 26 first.

Bible

Read out Genesis 1 that talks about God creating the world.

Talk

Explain that God is an amazing God and he alone created the world! We need to look after everything we see in the world: the land, the sea and the animals.

Game

In groups of three or four think of as many ways as possible in which we can look after the planet – ideas such as picking up litter and recycling are good.

Image

Aim

To show that everyone is equal in God's eyes, and we are all special to him.

Games

Animals

Everyone sits on a chair in a circle. Each chair is given the name of an animal. The person who starts is on the elephant chair and is the most important person. On his/her left is the least important person. What they have to do is to mime out their animal and then another person's animal. If they get it wrong they go to the last chair and everyone moves up one seat. If the person whose animal has been mimed does not react quickly enough they have to move to the last chair and everyone moves up a chair. The animal mime does not move with the person – it stays on the chair so that the group needs to remember which chair has which animal mime attached to it. The idea is to get each other out so that they go to the end and to get to the elephant chair, which is the most important one.

The price is right

For this you need two or three items from your home and the group has to try and guess how much each item is worth. Then read out a list of chemicals – magnesium, sulphur, water, phosphorous, iron, fat, lime and potash. Ask the group what they are worth in total. See who gets the closest (they all add up to approximately £7.99). Then explain that these are the components that make up a human being. In your body you have enough:

   Fat for seven bars of soap
   Iron for a medium-sized nail
   Sugar for seven cups of coffee

Lime to whitewash a dog kennel
Phosphorous to make 2200 match tips
Magnesium to make a dose of salts
Potash to blow up a toy train
Sulphur to rid a dog of fleas
Water to fill six buckets

Talk

Say that we put so much value on worldly things such as the valuables you showed, yet so little value on people. The chemicals are only worth a few pounds, about £7.99 in total; so little compared to the valuables, but these chemicals are what make up human beings! You cannot put a price on a person. Everyone is priceless and equal! Unlike the animal game we are all important.

Game

Newspaper fashion
Divide into small groups and give each group some newspapers. They have to design clothes for someone in the group to wear. After five minutes have a fashion parade and see who has won.

Bible bit

Read out Matthew 6:25-31 and Romans 10:12-13: Explain to the group the passage which says, 'Do not worry what to wear, we are all equal in God's eyes and you are special to him'.

Game

Lipstick
Choose four volunteers. The two boys sit down and two girls stand opposite them with lipstick between their lips. Without using their hands they try to put lipstick on the two boys' lips as accurately as possible.

Disability

Aim

To show that we need to think of other people who are less able bodied and understand their situation in order to help them.

Game

Jump kangaroo

Ask the group to stand in a circle. You stand in the middle with a large rope in your hand. As you swing the rope along the group all of them have to jump over the rope. If the rope catches their legs they are out. Continue until you have a winner.

Talk

Explain to the group what a privilege it is to have all your limbs in working order – to be able to walk, run and jump. Sometimes we take this privilege for granted. We need to think of others who are less fortunate than us.

Games

Face push

Divide the group into two teams. Each team has to form a line behind each other. On the word 'GO' the two in front must kneel down, put their hands behind their backs and with their faces push a football towards the other end of the room. When the ball hits the other end (or a target) they can run back to their team and the next person goes. Continue until you have a winning team.

Apple string

Produce two apples each with a piece of string through the middle and knotted under the apple. Ask for four volunteers. Two of the volunteers stand on chairs. They have to hold up the apple on a string. The other two have to put their hands behind their backs and using just their mouths they have one minute to see who can eat the most apple. This is a very hard game but it can be done.

Talk

Explain how difficult the last two games were – the first one was difficult because you couldn't use your feet to kick the ball – the second because you couldn't use your hands. Imagine what it would be like never to be able to use your limbs. Challenge the group to think about people who are disabled – to understand their situation and to think of ways of helping them.

Game

Mouth paint

Choose two volunteers. Sit them down in front of a table with a piece of paper and paint pot on it. Give them a paint brush which they have to put in their mouth. On the word 'GO' they have to paint whatever you tell them to, using just their mouth. See who is the best.

Conclusion

Say that many people who are disabled still manage to do some amazing things such as paint beautiful pictures with their mouth and a paint brush. Don't give up on people just because they may not be able to do what we can. God can use anyone, no matter what their situation.

Poverty trap

Aim

To show that we are really prosperous in this country compared to some people in the world. We need to think about others who don't have all that we have.

Games

Tramps' tea party

All the members sit in a circle facing each other. In the middle of the circle is a plate, knife and fork, bar of chocolate, hat, scarf and gloves. Give one of the members the dice. They have to roll the dice – if they get a six they can put on the clothes and start eating the chocolate with the knife and fork. As soon as someone else gets a six then they can grab the clothes off the person and take over eating the chocolate.

Banana game

Blindfold three members; when they are blindfolded give them two bananas each. Tell them that they are only allowed to use their left hand and that they have to race each other and eat the bananas as quickly as possible. As they start eating take the blindfold off one and whisper that they can use both hands and give them an extra banana. Unfair or what!?

Talk

Say that life can be cruel. In the first game some members were privileged and got some of the chocolate, others didn't get any. Just as they were about to eat the chocolate they got pulled away without eating any. Life for many people is like that: they have to sit and watch while others fill themselves with food. They starve and as soon as they get some food, it is gone!! They get it taken away from them often by those who already have more than enough, as in the banana game; they are also treated unfairly compared to others – *but* there is a challenge we need to take up. How can we help others who do not have enough? (For example, suggest buying Fair Trade produce.)

Activity

Divide the members into groups of five or six. In groups write down as many different ways of helping those in need, such as sponsored events. After five minutes read some of the suggestions and see how many your group can do.

Game

Give each member two cream crackers. On the word 'GO' they have to race by eating the crackers as fast as possible until they have finished. Use this game to emphasise how we fill ourselves with food whilst others go without.

Christmas

Aim

To show the true meaning of Christmas.

Games

Guess the meaning

Read out a word and give three different explanations for that word. The group has to decide which explanation they think is the correct one. Those who choose the wrong explanation are out. The winners are those who guess correctly.

Christmas

Ask the group what Christmas is all about and then in groups of three or four write down as many things to do with Christmas as possible. The group with the most things wins.

Story

Tell the story of the Nativity. Read some appropriate verses from one of the Gospels to back this up, or do a drama in groups.

Game

Two volunteers are blindfolded and have to wrap a present using wrapping paper, as quickly as possible. The winner is the one who wraps the present up the neatest.

Talk

Whilst Christmas has so many different meanings to people, such as parties, presents, food, families, etc., the true meaning is the 'birth of

Jesus'. This is often forgotten as people think about all those other things, like the 'wrappings' of Christmas, the secular things. As in the 'present wrap' game there was nothing special on the outside – he wasn't born in a palace but in a dirty old stable. But he was God's present to mankind.

Game

Gurgle a carol

Finish by choosing two volunteers. They have to drink some cola and gurgle a carol. The first one to have their carol guessed correctly – wins. Then choose two more volunteers.

What is a Christian?

Aim

To think about what a Christian is.

Group activity

Divide the group into teams of two or three. Then give each team a piece of paper and a pen. They have three minutes to write down as many things as possible that relate to the word Christian. See who has the most.

Game

Word association

Give two volunteers a subject like food. They have to say a word each that relates to that subject (food). Each word they say has to relate to the last word spoken. After a few tries give them the word 'Christianity'.

Talk

Ask someone from the local church or a youth group to share their story of how they became a Christian, or use a video clip of someone famous giving their testimony.

Game

Inside out

Give out after-dinner mints that come in little envelopes then give the group a puzzle. They have to try to turn the envelope inside out without tearing it – it can be done. If you don't have any after-dinner mints then use an ordinary envelope.

Talk

Tell the group that it may seem impossible to turn the envelope inside out but it can be done. The same goes for us, being a Christian is brilliant because God can forgive us and turn us inside out and totally change us. He can change us in our attitude and character and our thinking.